Polar Bear and Grizzly Bear

Rod Theodorou and Carole Telford

RIGBY
INTERACTIVE
LIBRARY

This edition © 1997 Rigby Education
Published by Rigby Interactive Library,
an imprint of Rigby Education,
division of Reed Elsevier, Inc.
500 Coventry Lane
Crystal Lake, IL 60014

Printed in Britain

Library of Congress Cataloging-in-Publication Data
Theodorou, Rod.
        Polar bear and grizzly bear / Rod Theodorou and Carole Telford.
            p.   cm. — (Discover the difference)
        Includes index.
        Summary: Compares and contrasts the physical attributes, habits, and
    habitat of polar bears and grizzly bears.
        ISBN 1-57572-105-8
        1. Polar bear—Juvenile literature. 2. Grizzly bear—Juvenile literature. [1. Polar
    bear. 2. Grizzly bear. 3. Bears.] I. Telford, Carole, 1961–   . II. Title. III. Series:
    Theodorou, Rod. Discover the difference.
    QL737.C27T48 1996
    599.74'446—dc20   96-7244

Designed by Susan Clarke
Illustrations by Adam Abel, Jeff Edwards, and Angela Owen

Acknowledgments
The publisher would like to thank the following for permission to reproduce photographs: Frank Huber/
Oxford Scientific Films, pp. 3 *top*, 20 *bottom*; Norbert Rosing/Oxford Scientific Films, pp. 3 *bottom*, 9, 19;
Tim Davis/Oxford Scientific Films, p. 5; Brian Kenney/Planet Earth Pictures, p. 7; Pat and Tom Leeson/
Oxford Scientific Films, p. 8; Daniel Cox/Oxford Scientific Films, pp. 10 *top*, 20 *top*; Mike Birkhead/
Oxford Scientific Films, p. 10 *bottom*; Silvestris/FLPA, pp. 11 *top*, 21; Gary Bell/Planet Earth Pictures, p. 11
bottom; Stouffer Productions/Oxford Scientific Films, pp. 12, 16; Nikita Ovsyanikov/Planet Earth Pictures,
p. 13 *top*; Dan Guravich/ Oxford Scientific Films, p. 13 *bottom*; W. Wisniewski/FLPA, p. 14 *top*; Bob
Bennett/Oxford Scientific Films, p. 14 *bottom*; Planet Earth Pictures, pp. 15, 17 *top*; L. Lee Rue/FLPA, p. 18.

Cover photographs reproduced with permission of W. Wisniewski/FLPA, *top*; Planet Earth Pictures,
bottom.

> **Note to the Reader**
> Some words in this book are printed in **bold** type. This indicates that the word is
> listed in the glossary on page 24. The glossary gives a brief explanation of words
> that may be new to you and tells you the page on which each word first appears.

Contents

Introduction

Bears are the largest meat-eating land animals on earth. Bears are very strong. They have short, powerful legs, and thick, shaggy fur. Bears have large teeth and long curved claws to help them eat all sorts of food. Bears eat roots, nuts, leaves, fruit, and—of course—honey. The polar bear is the only bear that eats mostly meat. There are not many other kinds of food where polar bears live.

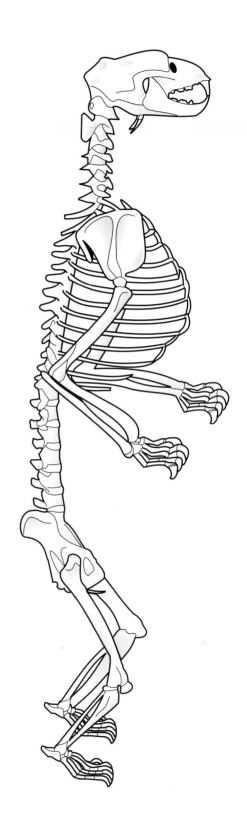

Bear skeletons are quite similar to human skeletons. Bears have large brains and are very intelligent.

Bears are mammals. They give birth to live young that look like smaller versions of themselves and feed them milk. There are seven different kinds of bear. The sun bear is the smallest bear. The largest bears of all are the big brown bears, including the grizzlies. Full-grown big brown bears can weigh about 500 pounds.

American black bear

Sun bear

Sloth bear

Spectacled bear

Grizzly bear

Asiatic black bear

Polar bear

The seven different kinds of bear are shown above.

Habitat

Many years ago, grizzly bears lived all over western North America. Over the last 150 years, thousands of grizzlies have been killed. Hunters and farmers kill the bears for meat, to protect their animals, or for sport. Today, most grizzlies live in Alaska and northern Canada.

This map shows where most grizzly bears and polar bears live today.

Where polar bears live.

Where grizzly bears live.

Polar bears have fur on the bottoms of their feet to keep them warm and stop them from slipping!

Polar bears live only in the far north in the frozen Arctic, an area around the North Pole. They are one of the few animals able to live in this land of ice and snow. Polar bears hunt on land and in the water. They usually eat seals.

In the 1950s, hunters shot hundreds of polar bears from airplanes. In 1973, five countries signed an agreement to stop the hunting.

Fur and Fat

Grizzly bears are among the largest of the big brown bears. They are called "grizzly" bears because some of them have silvery gray fur on their backs, which makes them look grizzly and old. Many grizzly bears don't have this coloring—they have dark brown or reddish-brown fur.

You can tell a grizzly bear from other brown bears by the hump of fat and muscle above its shoulders.

Polar bears are huge bears, too. They are twice as heavy as a male lion! Polar bears have long, thick coats, as well as a thick layer of fat under their skin to keep them warm. Their skin is black, but their fur is white. The Polar bear's white fur is the same color as snow, making it hard for their **prey** to see them.

A polar bear's fur grows especially thick in winter.

It's amazing!

A polar bear can have up to 3 inches of fat under its skin to help it keep warm.

Teeth, Claws, and Paws

Grizzly bears have broad, strong heads and big, sharp teeth. They also have powerful paws and sharp claws. Grizzly bears can kill a deer with a single blow from their paw. Grizzlies also use their paws to dig for roots, to scratch open ant nests, and to catch fish.

Few animals would dare to attack an adult grizzly bear!

A grizzly's front paws have huge curved claws.

Polar bears have sharper teeth than grizzlies, because they eat more meat. Their claws are sharp too, to help them grip slippery seals. Polar bears are excellent swimmers. They swim with their front paws and steer with their back legs. Polar bears keep their eyes open underwater, but they can close their nostrils!

Polar bears are expert hunters.

It's amazing!

A polar bear's large paws make it easy to walk on soft snow. Its front paws have skin between the toes to help it to swim fast.

Polar bears are strong swimmers.

Food

Grizzly bears are **omnivores.** They eat fruit, leaves, roots, and the bark of trees as well as insects, fish, and such small animals as squirrels. Grizzly bears also eat dead animals. A very hungry grizzly bear might even kill a larger animal, such as a deer. In the fall, grizzlies fatten themselves up on berries and nuts so they can hibernate through the long winter.

A grizzly bear scares wolves away from a deer they have killed.

Adult walruses guard their pups against a hungry polar bear.

Polar bears are **carnivores**, or meat eaters. They only eat plants if they cannot find meat. There is very little plant life in the Arctic, but there are lots of seals. Seals are the main food in a polar bear's diet, but they also eat birds, crabs, and fish. They will eat dead animals that they find, like walruses or whales.

It's amazing!

When food is scarce, grizzly and polar bears look for food in garbage dumps. The sugary food that they find makes their teeth rot!

A polar bear eats a seal it has killed.

Hunting

Grizzly bears are very good at catching fish. Scientists think that grizzly bears grow so big because of all the **protein** in the fish they eat. When **salmon** swim upstream each year, grizzly bears who live nearby have a feast! They gather by the river and wade into the water. As the salmon leap out of the water, the grizzlies catch them with their teeth. They also flip salmon out of the water and onto land with their paws.

A grizzly snatches a salmon out of the air.

It's amazing!

Grizzlies use their claws to strip the flesh off the fish they catch, leaving the whole skeleton behind!

Polar bears have to be good
hunters to catch seals. Seals need
air while they are under water, so
they make breathing holes in the
ice. A polar bear will wait for hours
by a breathing hole, knowing a seal
will come up for air. The polar bear
sneaks up on the seal by crawling
on its belly and then pouncing!

It's amazing!

When a polar bear is
hunting a seal, it will
cover its black nose
with its white paw
to stay hidden!

Hibernation

Grizzly bears make **dens** in caves or under tree roots. In the winter months, when food is hard to find, the grizzlies stay in their dens to **hibernate**, or sleep. During this "winter sleep," grizzly bears don't even wake up to eat or drink. They live off the fat they have stored in their bodies.

A grizzly bear pulls leaves into its den.

It's amazing!
Unlike other animals that hibernate in winter, grizzlies can wake up quickly to defend themselves if disturbed.

A polar bear and her cub stand at the entrance of their den.

A polar bear has dug this den.

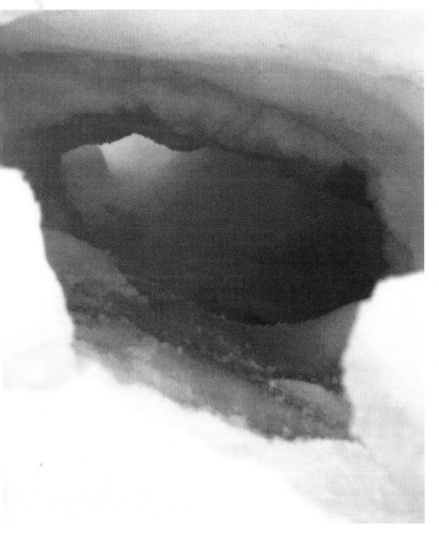

Polar bears make a den only if the winter is worse than usual. A **pregnant** polar bear will also make a den. They dig through a deep drift of snow with their powerful claws. Once inside, their fat and fur keep them warm. Even if the den gets covered in thick snow, it is safe inside.

Cubs

Grizzly bear **cubs** are born in their mother's den. Usually, the mother has only two cubs at a time. She spends all winter in the den looking after them. She has nothing to eat or drink during this time. Even though they will grow into huge adult bears, when cubs are born they are only about the size of an adult rabbit.

This grizzly cub is 10 days old, but still has its eyes and ears closed.

Leaves and twigs help keep a grizzly bear's den warm.

Polar bear cubs are almost twice the size of grizzly bear cubs when they are born. Polar bear cubs stay in the den all winter too, snuggling up to the mother to keep warm. As the cubs get stronger and more active, the mother digs out snow to make more room for the cubs to play.

It's amazing!

If winter snow buries the den too deeply, the mother digs an air hole to the surface.

These polar bear cubs are suckling milk from their mother.

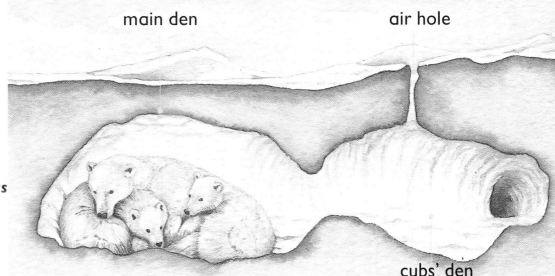

main den

air hole

This polar bear den has an air hole.

cubs' den

Growing up

In the spring, the mother grizzly bear leads her cubs out of the den. The cubs stay with her for two to four years, learning how to find food and catch fish. Bears have good memories. Cubs soon know what is good to eat. Cubs spend a lot of time playing and running to make their muscles strong.

A female grizzly and her cubs look for berries.

Grizzly cubs are quite playful.

Polar bear cubs stay with their mother for about two years. The cubs follow her as she looks for seals. The cubs learn how to hunt seals by watching her. They soon learn to be very still while their mother is hunting. If they move, they might scare the seal away!

A young polar bear follows its mother across the pack ice.

It's amazing!

If a cub moves around while its mother is hunting, she may swat it with her powerful paw!

Fact File

Grizzly Bear

Weight
Grizzly bears can weigh up to 900 pounds.

Length
Grizzlies grow to about 8 feet long.

Habitat
Grizzlies live in Alaska, northern Canada, and parts of Idaho, Montana, Washington, and Wyoming.

Food
Grizzly bears eat roots, nuts, berries, bark, fruit, leaves, insects, birds, fish, small animals, dead animals, and sometimes a large animal like a deer.

Polar Bear

Weight
Polar bears weigh up to 1,000 pounds.

Length
Polar bears grow to $8\frac{1}{2}$ feet long.

Habitat
Polar bears live in areas in the Arctic, including parts of Canada, Greenland, Russia, and Alaska.

Food
Polar bears eat seals, young walruses, small animals, eggs, grass and other plants, and dead animals.

Glossary

carnivore an animal that eats other animals   **13**

cub baby bear   **18**

den animal's shelter   **16**

hibernate to sleep through the winter   **16**

omnivore animal that eats plants and animals   **12**

pack ice large, floating pieces of ice   **21**

pregnant carrying a baby inside the body   **17**

prey animal hunted or caught for food   **9**

protein nutrients found in such food as eggs, milk, fish, and meat   **14**

salmon large fish that swims from salt water to fresh water each year to lay eggs   **14**

Index

Further Readings

Markert, Jenny. *Polar Bears*. Child's World Wildlife Library, 1991.

Patent, Dorothy Hinshaw. *Looking at Bears*. Holiday House, 1994.

Stirling, Ian (text) and Aubrey Lang, (photos). *Bears*. Sierra Club Books for Children, 1992.